04 패턴의 구성
Pattern Components

JN452008

가디건용 패턴
Cardigan Patterns

시보리용 패턴은 생략

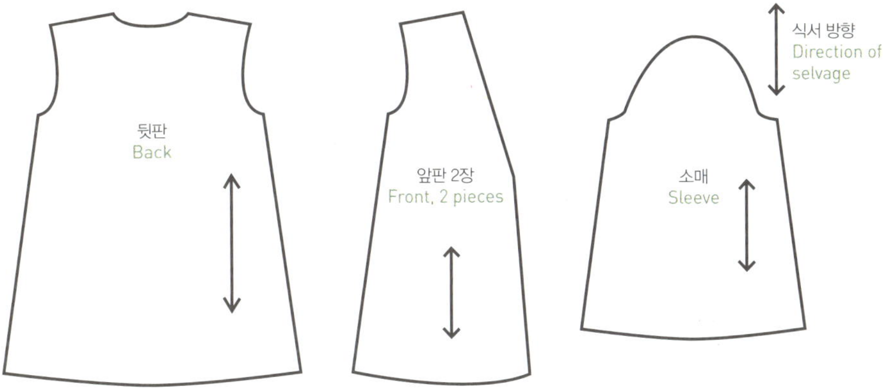

티셔츠용 패턴
T-shirt Patterns

스커트용 패턴
Skirt Patterns

체크 스커트 상단용 1장 Upper Layer of checkered skirt, 1 piece

체크 스커트 하단용(속지용) 1장 Lower Layer (Underskirt) of checkered skirt, 1 piece

식서 방향 Direction of selvage

프릴용 패턴 Pattern for the Frill

체크 프릴용 2장 for checkered frill, 2 pieces

검정 T/C 프릴용 1장 for the black TC frill, 1 piece

골선 Crease Line

참고) 골선은 원단을 접어서 재단하는 경우로 재단하여 펼치면 2배의 길이가 됩니다.

Note: Please notice that the actual length will double on unfolding, as the fabric is folded along the crease line before cut.

속바지용 패턴
Underpants Patterns

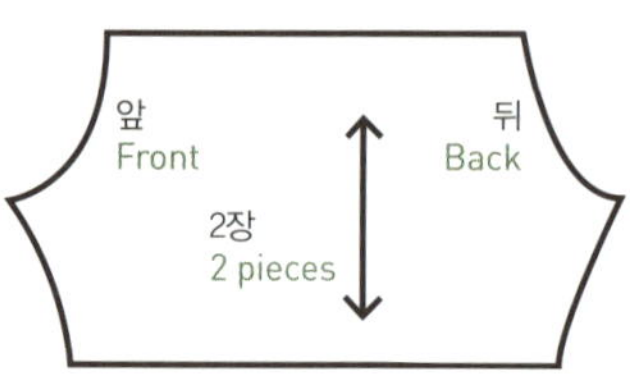

식서 방향 Direction of selvage

스타킹용 패턴
Stocking Pattern

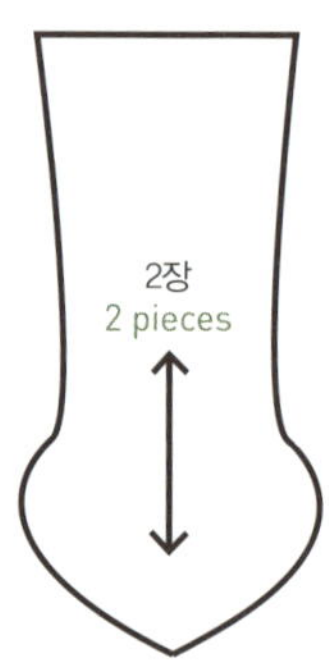

식서 방향 Direction of selvage

05 가디건 만들기
Making the Cardigan

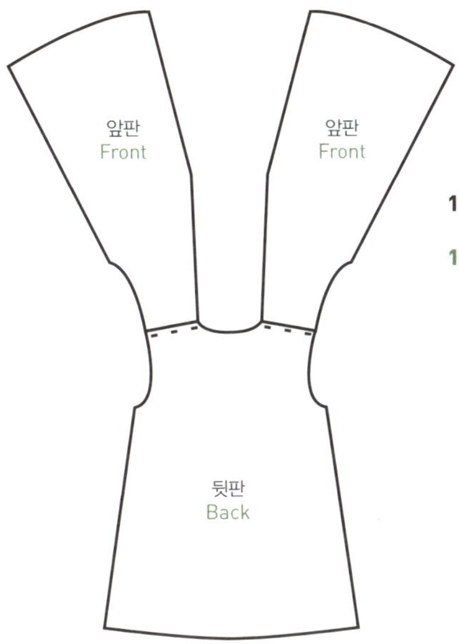

1. 가디건 뒷판에 앞판 2장의 어깨 솔기를 박아 시접을 뒷판쪽으로 시접처리하여 넘긴다.

1. Sew the two Cardigan Fronts onto the Cardigan Back along the shoulder seam with a margin, and trim the seam allowance backwards.

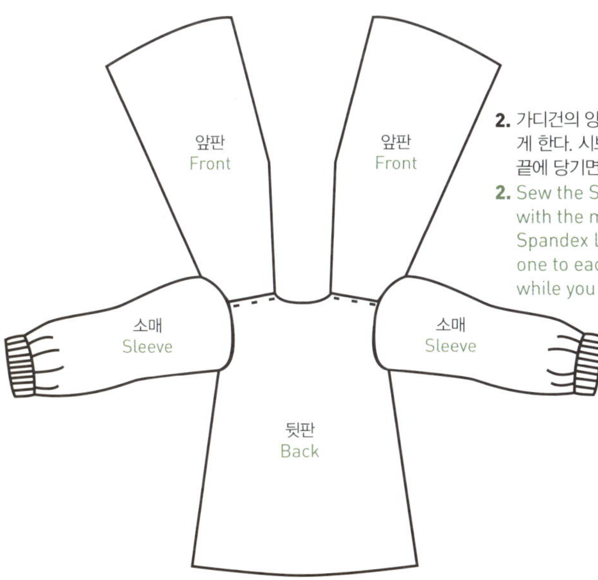

2. 가디건의 양쪽 소매를 달고 시접을 소매쪽으로 향하게 한다. 시보리는 3cm×8cm 2장을 잘라 양쪽 소매 끝에 당기면서 달아준다.

2. Sew the Sleeves onto the cardigan bodice with the margin toward the Sleeves. Cut two Spandex Linings of 1½"×3½" size and sew one to each of the sleeve hem, stretching while you sew them.

3. 앞판과 뒷판을 마주보게 포개어 밑쪽부터 소매쪽으로 양쪽(화살표방향)을 박어 시접처리한다.

3. Put the Cardigan Fronts and Back facing inside; sew up from the bottom upwards, then downward the sleeve, as the arrows show. Sew at both sides, and trim the margin.

4. 가디건의 밑단을 시보리용(예 : two by one 스판)을 세로 3cm×가로 20cm 정도 잘라 댕겨가며 박은후 시접처리한다.

4. Cut the Spandex Lining into 1½"×8" size and sew it onto the hem of the cardigan, stretching softly. Trim the margin.

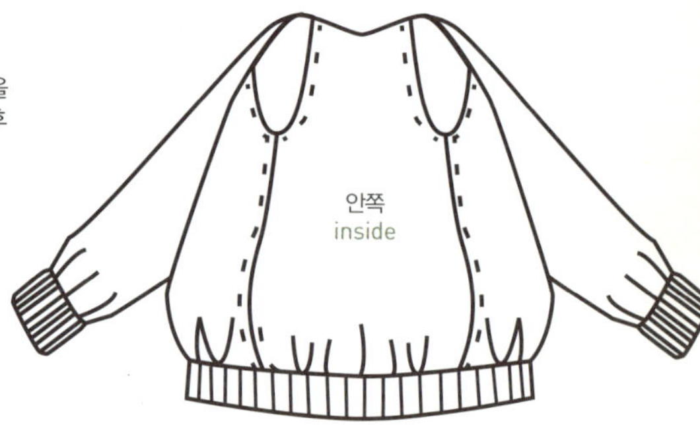

5. 시보리용(예 : two by one 스판)을 세로 3cm×가로 45cm 정도 잘라 밑단부터 침을 6곳 찔러 놓은 부분을 따라 자연스럽게 박고 겉에서 눌러준다.

5. Cut the Spandex Lining into 1½"×18" size before align it from the bottom by fixing it with 6 pins. Sew up and press from outside.

참고) 시보리는 늘어나는 천으로 자연스럽게 늘려 6곳 정도 고르게 침을 찔러 바느질하면 옷이 한쪽으로 쏠리지도 않고 편안하게 완성된다.

Note: Lining Layer with spandex fabric woven 2-thread by 1 thread assures easy stretching and tightening effect at the hem lining. If you fix it with pins at about 6 places before sewing, the garment wouldn't shrink on either side after finished.

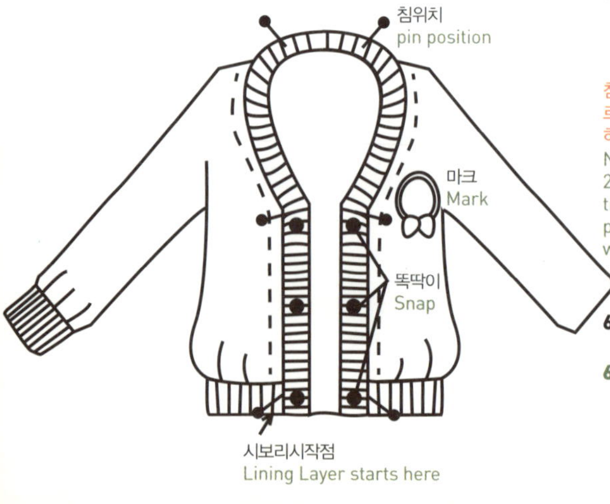

6. 가디건 왼쪽에 장식용 마크와 리본을 달아준다. 앞여임에 똑딱이 단추 3쌍도 달아준다.

6. Stitch the Mark and the Ribbon on the left side of the Cardigan Front for decoration. Stitch 3 pairs of snaps onto the front opening.

06 티셔츠 만들기
Making the T-shirt

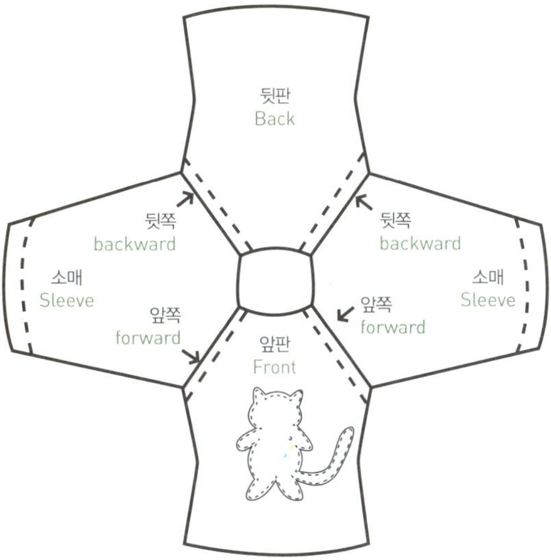

1. 앞판과 뒷판을 구분하여 나그랑 소매를 달아 시접처리를 하여 몸쪽으로 넘겨 눌러박아 준다.
앞판에 장식용 인형을 박아준다. 핫픽스용 장식을 다리미로 눌러 주어도 예쁘다. 소매밑단은 시접처리후 1cm정도 꺾어 눌러 박는다.

1. Put Raglan Sleeve to the corresponding position and sew up with a margin. Trim the margin toward the bodice.
Sew the Doll Picture on the Shirt Front for decoration. Or you may want to decorate a hot fix ornament, which also looks nice, by pressing with the iron. Trim the Sleeve hem before tuck in ½" and sew while pressing gently.

참고) 앞쪽보다 나그랑 소매의 길이가 더 길다.
Note: Please notice that the Sleeve is longer than the Shirt Front.

2. 가디건과 동일하게 앞뒷판을 포개어 몸쪽 밑단부터 소매 쪽으로 눌러 박는다.

2. Put the Shirt Front and Back facing inside, as you did the cardigan, and sew up from the bottom upwards, then down the sleeve. Press while you sew.

3. 20's 면과 스커트용 체크천으로 모자용 패턴을 2장씩 떠서 2장씩 포개어 박은후 20's면 모자와 체크용 모자의 겉과 겉을 놓고 포개박은후 뒤집어 눌러 박는다.

3. Cut two pairs of the Hood Pattern from the Cotton of 20s threads and also from the Checkered fabric for the skirt. Sew the 2 pieces of the same material together; once for the Cotton, and then for the Checkered. Then, put the two hoods surfaces facing inside, and sew them up. Turn the hood inside side out to sew up, pressing.

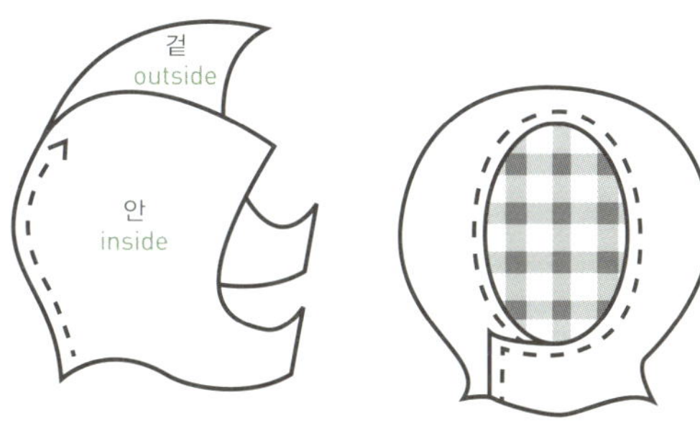

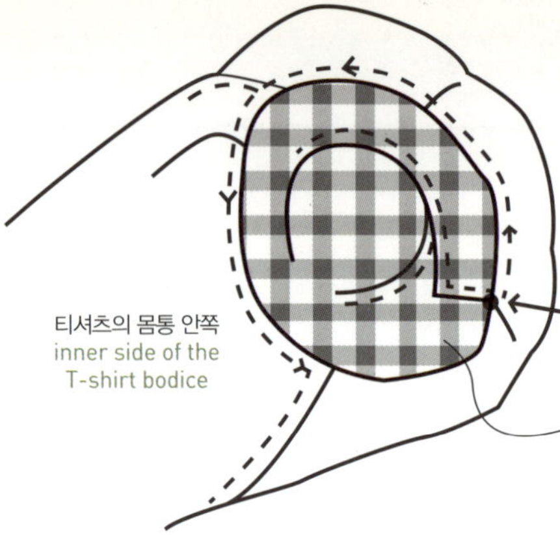

4. 티셔츠의 안쪽 뒷판 중심에 체크쪽 모자 뒷중심을 맞춘후 앞판 나그랑 끝지점에서 모자를 박기 시작하여 원으로 편안하게 박는다.

4. Join the T-Shirt Back and Hood at the middle of the inner side of the Shirt Back and the middle of the Hood back of the Checkered side; sew them up together starting from the Shirt Front at the edge of the Raglan Sleeve, in a circle.

5. 모자를 둥글게 박아 뒤집어 밑단을 시접처리한 후 꺾어 박는다. 똑딱이 1쌍과 단추 1개를 달아준다.

5. Sew the hood around, turn it inside out, trim the hem before you tuck in the margin and sew up. Stitch one pair of Snaps and one Button.

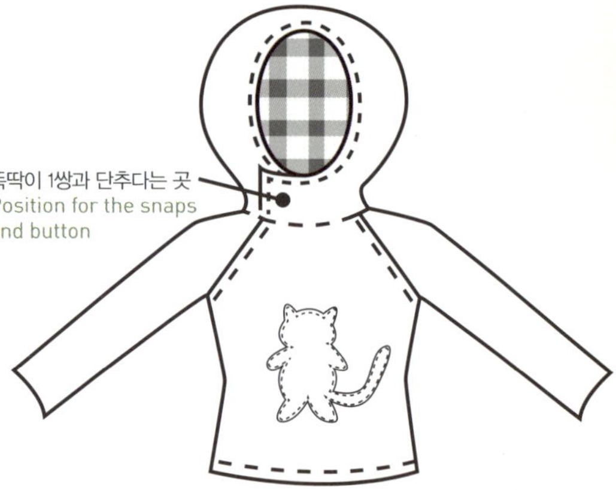

07 스커트 만들기 Making the Skirt

1. 체크스커트용 상단을 맨 밑에 놓고, 그 위에 체크 프릴을 놓고 체크 치마 하단용(속지)를 덮어 놓고 박는다.

1. Iron the concealed zipper(hidden fastener) and sew it at the back of the dress: or, snaps may do as well.

2. 박은 스커트를 뒤집어 체크프릴의 위쪽을 눌러 박은 후 치마 밑단에 검정 프릴을 골고루 펴 달아 준다. 박은후 시접처리하고 겉에서 눌러 박는다.

2. Turn the sewed-up skirt face side out and sew the checkered frill onto it along the upper side. Attach the Black TC Frill along the skirt hem, smoothing out evenly. Sew it up before trim the margin; then sew on the face side, pressing.

3. 스커트 맨 밑단의 검정 프릴이 약 2cm 정도 덮일정도로 빨강체크 프릴을 달고, 그와 같은 방법으로 균일하게 레이스 프릴을 달아 준다.

3. Join the Red Checkered Frill, overlapping the Black TC Frill about 1", sew up. Join and sew up the Black Lace Frill in the same way, smoothing evenly.

참고) 프릴은 시접처리한 후 눌러박고 주름노루발을 이용해 균일하게 주름을 만들어 사용한다.

Note: Before sewing the Frills, trim the margin. Sew it pressing, while making even frills using a shirring ruffler.

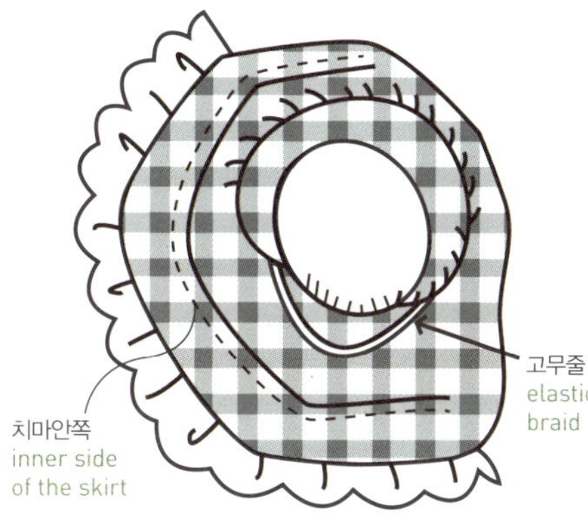

4. 스커트 양끝을 포개어 안쪽에서 박아 원으로 만든후에 안쪽에 고무줄(15cm 잘라 원으로 만듬)을 넣어가며 원으로 눌러박아 준다.

4. Join the opposite ends of the Skirt, sew up from inside, making it into a cylinder; then sew an elastic braid which you had cut in 6" length and made into a circle onto the skirt, pressing.

08 속바지 만들기
Making the Underpants

1. 재단된 속바지용 천 2장을 겉과 겉을 마주대고 안쪽에서 앞, 뒤를 마추어 박는다. 밑단은 레이스를 달아 눌러박은후 고무줄을 땡겨 박아준다.

1. Put the Underpants patterns with the face sides together, and sew from the inside, joining corresponding sides- front to front and back to back. Attach lace along the hem and sew while pressing. Then sew the elastic braid, stretching hard

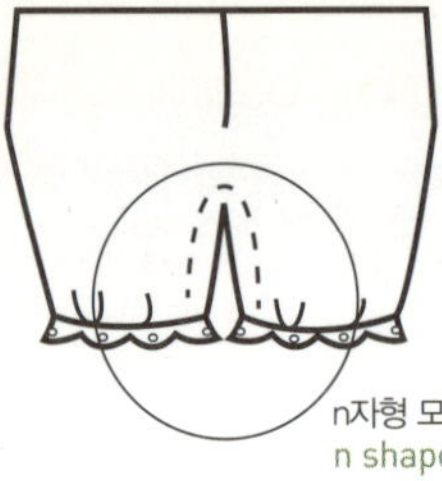

2. 앞, 뒤 중심을 놓고 가랑이를 'n'자형으로 박아 시접처리한다.

2. Join the Front and Back at the center, sew the crotch in a 'n' shape.

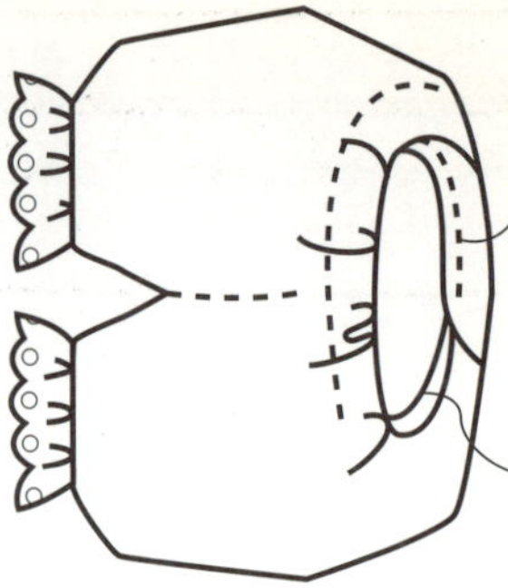

3. 고무줄을 15cm 잘라 원으로 박은후 속바지 상단에 고무줄을 넣어가며 원으로 박는다.

6. Cut the elastic braid in a 6" length cord and form a circle to sew it along the top of the underpants.

09 스타킹 만들기 Making the Stockings

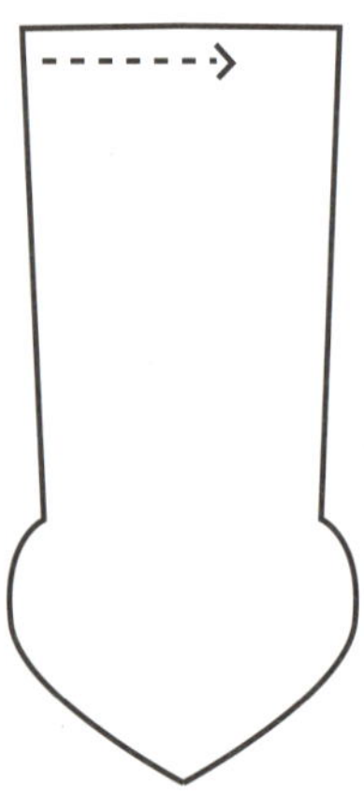

1. 위의 단을 늘려가며 박는다.

1. Sew around the top, stretching the hem.

2. 반접은 스타킹을 안쪽 위에서 아래로 박아준다.

2. Fold the Stocking and sew inside from the top to bottom.